MW00878136

The Magic of Accelerated Learning

Master Advanced Strategies for Improved Memory, Laser-sharp Focus & Quicker Learning, and Become An Expert Faster

Som Bathla

www.sombathla.com

Table of Contents

Chapter 1: Introduction

****

"The great breakthrough in your life comes when you realize that you can learn anything you need to learn to accomplish any goal that you set for yourself. This means there are no limits on what you can be, have, or do."

~ Brian Tracy

The other day, I was just looking back at my high school days.

It all seemed like I was watching some movie. I would consider myself a relatively introverted child since my childhood, though an inquisitive one. While my introverted nature made me sit with myself for hours, the inquisitive part of me kept on thinking why the things were the way they were. I knew that I wanted to explore many things in my life, but the irony of growing in a small town is that you don't have much infrastructure to quench your thirst of knowledge. Moreover, since I was born in a lower middle-class family, the opportunity to study in a reasonable school, play in the evening, and sleep with full stomach was luxury for us (of course, it is way better than those kids who had to work or help their parents in their work from an early age).

I remember I just had a limited number of friends with whom I could openly share my thoughts about my desire to explore ways to improve life, be it personal, financial, or just living better. Had there been internet in those days in India, I might have gotten my desire to explore satiated to good extent—but we only had access to random newspapers. As I grew into an adolescent, my quench for exploration made me write enquiry letters to various advertisements for mutual funds, insurance companies, educational institutions, professional development courses, etc. Since these organizations put their postal address in their advertisements for any queries, I used that opportunity to write letters to them enquiring about their products, programs, fee structure, and how I could benefit from their product or services.

You might laugh at me—a kid writing letters to mutual funds companies seeking more details about their products when he didn't have a penny to invest. But I was getting responses from those companies— maybe they didn't want to lose a potential customer or maybe they'd have just ignored me had they been aware that it was just a curious kid on the other side. Anyway, I was feeling special that such big companies were giving me a response. Also, when frequent letters by post used to arrive home addressed in my name, my siblings were surprised (and also somewhat inspired) to see the sheer volume of newsletters and magazines I have collected over some time.

During my first college days, besides my studies, I was trying to learn and understand other topics, like the stock market, how a cooperation operates and made profits, and trying to be aware of the trends. But these newsletters, information brochures, and catalogues raised another problem: it was too much information for me. I realized that though I was curious and able to find the information, I wasn't able to fully retain the information for future use.

My drive for exploration pushed me to buy my first ever skill enhancement book. It was a book about mind power study techniques for enhancing my learning skills. The book had good material, and it helped me with few techniques to learn and understand better. Moreover, I also worked with some other intelligent students in my class to understand their style of learning and retention, and noted that they were following certain methodologies to learn better. Precisely all efforts on how to learn better were on my own, as generally most schools only required students to learn the subject matter, but not the best ways to learn.

Now time was flying. I completed college, my professional education, and then started working in the corporate world and those learning techniques helped me. My desire for learning stayed with me. Besides my professional work-related books, I surrounded myself with books on different topics. I was reading various types of literature from high profile business magazines like the *Economist* to thought-provoking business books on thinking, decision making, and learning better. Though I was consuming more information, there was still a nagging feeling in my mind that there could still be improved ways to accelerate my learning.

Though my earlier understanding of ways of learning was self-studied, it served me well throughout my life so far. But as you would have heard the saying: "What got you here won't get you there." Therefore, I became curious about learning the ways to learn better, faster, retain information for long-term, in order to improve my ability to retrieve the information—to make better decisions in my life. This is because I strongly believe that learning is not something that should stop after you finish college; rather it is a life-long process. The more I dove deeper into the subject, the more I realized that had these principles been known to me way back in my childhood, it would have significantly improved my capabilities. But anyways, it still gives me a sense of satisfaction that time I spent researching has equipped me with refined tools that will now remain with me for life to learn effectively. I sincerely hope that you will also benefit from the information and strategies that you are going to discover in this book.

Your Questions About Accelerated Learning

If you are reading about my personal experience, it seems you are at some level trying to connect with my story. Maybe you also have some questions about the ways to learn better, faster, and more effectively. Let me help you surface out some of your questions from the inner layers of your mind by listing some questions that I had been seeking answers to in my quest. You may have questions like:

- How does our brain's neural network and memory work, and what are the best ways to firmly store new pieces of information in our brain?
- Why do we forget information, and how could we develop our memory?
- What is the effectiveness of the learning methods that we have knowingly or unknowingly used so far in learning material?
- Have our schools or colleges ever taught us about the best ways to learn for long-term retention, or were we just forced to cram our test

material only to regurgitate it in an exam the next morning?

- What are the best ways to get maximum ROTI (return on time invested) in reading and learning new information (i.e. retain the most information so we can retrieve and make the best decisions out of that information).

- What are the tools or strategies that can help us retain information, and turn that information into our personal wisdom?

I don't know about your precise objective of learning the ways to learn faster and better, but I assume that you have resonated with some of the questions above. And if you stay with me, I promise you to provide you enough valuable techniques based on my positive experience of implementing them and many other strategies explored through my further research that will help you accelerate your learning process.

What Should You Expect Out Of This Book?

My approach is to provide maximum value to the reader. I want to pack this book with lots of information, and still want to keep it short. I have realized that nowadays most people don't look for detailed background, or full details with huge explanation of any subject. This is because people's attention spans have already shortened so much, thanks to the high-end technology and smartphones loaded with multiple social media apps. Therefore people are only concerned about the information that helps them solve their problem with the shortest possible investment of their time.

Therefore, I tend to keep all my books as reasonably short as possible. I see a win-win proposition for both readers and for myself as a writer. Readers read such books faster. And writers can write such books faster. To be candid with you, I write books to enhance my learning on different types of subjects. This is because one of the best ways of learning is to teach someone. (You will find a complete section on how teaching is proven to be one of the most effective techniques for learning). Therefore, whatever topics I find interesting and want to learn more about, I read and research about the topic, try to incorporate it into my life, and then start teaching that topic through my books.

So, this book will be short, but full of actionable information. More specifically, this book will cover:

- How your brain works and the role of memory in enhanced learning.
- Different types of learning strategies and how most commonly used strategies for learning are not that effective.
- Few less-known learning strategies for better comprehension and motivation.
- Myths about different learning styles and how you should take notes while learning something new.
- How you can learn by making learning a fun experience— gamification and challenges to help you to learn faster.
- Researched studies and use of technology to show how teaching someone is the best way to learn.
- Stages of learning and how to reach the top level of learning to become an expert in your field.

Chapter 2: How Do Our Brain And Memory Function?

****

"Your brain has a capacity for learning that is virtually limitless, which makes every human a potential genius." ~ **Michael J. Gelb**

The objective of learning faster requires careful examination of all the factors related to the process of learning. Human brain is the key infrastructure for imbibing any new learning. Therefore, we will first start with the **internal functioning of our brains**.

To be precise, learning at a very basic level is a biological function with our brain as the main component to facilitate this. Our brain is an ultra complex organ. When you are reading this page, you wouldn't realize how many functions your brain is handling at this single point of time. Your brain is instructing your eyes to read the words on this page, then after reading the images of the words, your brain is forming connections within itself to derive some meaning out of those words, which will then become your understanding of the concept.

Moreover, your brain is not merely occupied in reading this page. While reading, your brain is also doing a lot more functions within you and around you. You are smoothly breathing, and all the bodily functions inside your body are carried out at super quick (maybe millionth fraction of a second) instructions of your brain. Then on the outside, perhaps there are other things happening like the sound of the fan or air conditioner, maybe you get some fragrance or odor around you; your mind is filtering all those sounds and smells, to be unimportant. Your brain is ensuring that you remain focused on reading this page, while in the background it is efficiently handling many functions simultaneously. And all of this is happening at such a fast pace, that you even don't realize all this happening because our brain is possibly the most complex object known to us.

I guess you would now be interested in knowing the complex infrastructure inside the brain that facilitates learning.

Let's now get inside the brain to examine how our brains understand from the multitude of information consistently bombarding it every moment of life. Neuroscience studies show that the human brain has more than 100 billion neurons. Each neuron has a cell body with two components: (1) a single long branch known as *axon;* and (2) multiple shorter branches known as *dendrites* (see image).

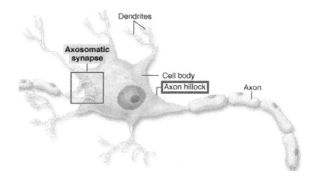

One important transaction that happens within the brain is when neurons pass on signals to the other neurons. They do it through touching other neurons, and that junction is called the *synapse*.

Current brain research supports the idea that most learning and development happens in the brain through the strengthening and weakening of these *synaptic connections*. There is some estimation that each neuron may have anywhere from one to ten thousand synaptic connections, and therefore the number of different patterns of possible connections in the brain is about forty quadrillion, a number that is beyond comprehension of a normal human being.

These neurons are the basic functional cells that appear to control learning. They encode, store, and retrieve information as well as influence all aspects of human behavior. Neurons act like tiny batteries sending chemical and electrical signals that create processes to integrate and generate information. The threshold for firing at the synapse is determined by the amount of chemicals (called neurotransmitters) released onto the receiving neurons (Bloom, Nelson, and Lazerson, 2001). At the synapse, these chemicals either excite the receiving neurons and cause them to fire, inhibit them from firing, or modify their excitability. Examples of common neurotransmitters are dopamine and epinephrine, which are involved in affecting our emotions and mood.

Whenever we learn something new, that information is stored in the brain through connection between different neurons. It is only through practice and repetition that we strengthen the connection between the neurons. In fact, neuroscientists have a cliché: Neurons that fire together wire together. Apparently, all our learning and information occurs through the connection between the neurons. For example, imagine that a neuron that encodes a place and another that encodes an emotion are activated when a wrong experience is felt at this particular place. As a result of this experience, these two neurons fire together and then wire together. Then, whenever the neurons of this particular place are activated, the emotion is also retrieved. Small networks are connected with other small and large networks to resemble a forest of neuronal networks with tens of thousands of synaptic connections.

Therefore, all our deeply held beliefs are nothing but the neuron connection, which we keep on strengthening by repetition of the older thoughts.

For any new learning to form in our brains, it is vital that the neurons fire a lot and make numerous synaptic connections, which only happens through consistent repetition and practice.

I am neither a neuroscientist nor a brain expert. The objective of this book is also not to give you some thesis on the anatomy of our brains. The idea of taking a quick peep inside your brain is to give you some brief update about the internal infrastructure and invisible function happening within our brains that facilitate learning.

It would also be better here to have a broad understanding of one other important aspect of learning: memory

What Is the Role of Memory in the Learning Process?

Let's first understand what memory is.

According to the Oxford Dictionary, memory is defined as *"the mental capacity of holding evidences, actions, imitations, and so forth or recollecting earlier practices."*

"Memory is the means by which we draw on our past experiences in order to use this information in the present." (Sternberg, 1999)

Functionally, memory is defined as the capability to encode, hold, and subsequently remember material in the brain. From a psychological and neurological viewpoint[1], memory is the collection of encoded neural connections in the brain. It is the rebuilding of previous happenings and practices by a synchronous firing of neurons that were fired at the time of learning.

Our memory plays a key role in any new learning. After all, what is the use of learning anything new when you are not able to retrieve the information at the required time.

Some people would argue that you don't need a good memory in this modern age.

---

[1]

https://pdfs.semanticscholar.org/b621/7be7df0969f8f2c e6decb332c1ddbf896827.pdf

They would say that when all information is accessible by merely searching through Google, why would you fill your mind with information and data. I used to think that way for a long time. But thankfully, I realized that there are times that you are not in a position to look at Google to get answers. Moreover, making quicker decisions in complex scenarios requires you to have the relevant facts and information securely stored in your head. Having a stronger memory facilitates quicker decision-making, as you can quickly process the data in your brain and come out with the solution.

High-performers in any field, be it corporate, politics, or any other aspect of life, don't jump on to Google to look for most answers. Rather, they have strengthened their memory in a way that helps them to retrieve information in the real time, and when it is most needed.

Ken Jennings, a celebrity game show contest and author once said,

"When you make a decision, you need facts. If those facts are in your brain, they're at your fingertips. If they're all in

Google somewhere, you may not make the right decision on the spur of the moment."

Memory is therefore very crucial to learning. We can say that **memory** is a storage system formed within specific neural pathways, while **learning** is all about changing those old neural pathways and thus altering the thinking and behavior of a person through the infusion of new information. Learning and memory are closely connected, because the objective of the learning is to imbibe new knowledge into our memory. New memory formed through learning will in turn help us to make better decisions.

Memorization is the process through which we store and retrieve information for use later when we need it. That's what is required in the process of learning anything new. There are three steps to creating a memory.

1. Encoding
2. Storage
3. Retrieval

Encoding is processing the information from your all senses. You are processing information every time in all manners. While reading, you process information by seeing through your eyes. While listening, touching, or smelling, you are exposing yourself to some information to process through your brain. Therefore, encoding is an input process.

Storage is the process of storing the information in the neural pathways of our brains. How much information one can store is dependent upon the efforts that went into encoding and how important the information is. In the coming sections, we will learn about the best ways to encode the information in a way that helps to strengthen the storage of information in our brains.

Retrieval is the most important function and objective of our memory. Whenever you need the information, you should be in a position to recall the information and put it to use—and that's the objective of retrieval. Retrieval of information is the output.

This section's objective was to briefly outline the basic tenets of learning faster. First, you need to understand the function of your brain, therefore, we looked at the deeper layers of the brain to understand the operating system of our brains. Secondly, we also discussed the concept of memory, as it is the necessary mechanism to retain any new learning in our brains.

In the next sections, we will talk about the important learning techniques with the pros and cons of each technique and the best ways to retain the information in your brain.

Chapter 3: Effective Strategies for Better Comprehension and Sustainable Memory

****

"Learning how to learn is one of the most important life skills." ~ Norma Fauziyah

Do you recall any specific classes or instructions during your school days, where they taught you how to learn effectively and in a way that sustains?

I don't remember being taught about the best ways to learn. We were simply given the subject matter to be learned and we had to figure out intuitively the way to learn. The methods I remember using in the childhood to learn was cramming most of the time (at least for theoretical subjects like history or geography) for examinations. Though this method served the immediate purpose of passing the exams well, but frankly I don't remember the years in which different battles were fought, nor do I remember which crops were grown where, or different species of animals living in the ocean. Maybe that information is not relevant for our day-to-day living, maybe we are not interested in those subjects, or maybe there was some defect in our learning methods. We will cover various methods in detail in this section.

Another way I recall was to learn by just forcing my mind to recall the information through hiding with my hand the answers to the questions that I just read. Most of you would also recollect learning through re-reading the information to store the information in your memory. We still do a lot of this now. Some people highlight the sentences in the books that they think are important and worth remembering–with the assumption that highlighted information would stick in their brain (research proves that it is an ineffective way. More on that later in this section).

We are used to using these various ways to learn, but the key concern is that though we use these different techniques, we are not sure of the efficacy of the ways of learning. We are always being informed of what we need to learn, but never has there been any greater emphasis on how we should learn. So we just keep going with our accidentally adopted techniques without ever checking the efficacy of the techniques.

That's why we wonder why most of the information we try to learn in our day-to-day lives don't seem to stick in our brains. It is our brain's natural tendency to forget things, unless there are calculated steps taken to retain the information in our brains longer. To start, let's learn something about why we forget.

Why Do We Forget?

Researcher H.F. Spitzer submitted a research paper[2] at State University of Iowa wherein he conducted an experiment to test how much information a person is able to retain in his memory if he learns the textbook material (without using any memory methods). The results show that the subjects were able to remember only the following:

After 1 day: 54%

---

[2] http://www.gwern.net/docs/spacedrepetition/1939-spitzer.pdf

After 7 days: 35%

After 14 days: 21%

After 21 days: 19%

After 28 days: 18%

The results mean that an average student is able to remember only 18% of his work after a gap of 28 days. After a 28-day vacation, the teacher has to start teaching his students again who have 18% retention of information, not 100%. That's where it was aptly quoted below:

"You know as well as I do that it is entirely wrong to assume that any subject matter which we once learned and mastered will remain our mental property forever."
~Bruno Furst

To reflect the above tendency to forget, German psychologist Hermann Ebinghaus, a pioneer in the experimental study of memory, coined the concept of **Forgetting Curve**. The forgetting curve explains the hypothesis of the decline in memory retention with the passage of time. The picture below explains the concept of the forgetting curve, and it shows how after learning information, we lose the information in a matter of couple of days or weeks, if there are no attempts made to retain it.

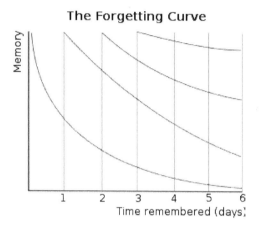

(Image courtesy: Wikipedia)

A related concept is the strength of memory that refers to the durability of memory traces in our brains. The stronger the memory, the longer the person is able to retain the memory. The graph above shows that typically humans tend to significantly lose the newly learned knowledge from their memory in a matter of days unless they consciously review the learned material.

Suppose, as a student, you read some information about people, places or other facts about the Second World War today for the first time and then don't make any attempt to revise or recollect the information by the end of the week. You will lose more than half of the information.

There are two key concerns that I want to highlight here that become hindrances in solidifying our learning and retaining the information in our brains. One, we are not sure that we are using the best ways to learn something new. This results in a waste of significant amount of our precious time due to not using the right methodology to learn. The second area of concern is most people are either ignorant or don't pay attention to the tendency of forgetting, thanks to the theory of the forgetting curve.

Ebbinghaus also discovered the concept of spacing effect in relation to the strengthening of the memory. The **spacing effect** is the phenomenon whereby learning is greater when studying is spread out over time, as opposed to studying the same amount of content in a single session.

It means it is better to use spaced presentation rather than massed presentation (you will learn more about these later in this section). Practically, this effect suggests that "cramming" (intense, last-minute studying solely to address the examination) the night before an exam is not likely to be as effective as studying at intervals in a longer time frame. Though you will not see the greater results of spaced repetition in the shorter duration, this has a sustainable effect in retention of information in our memories.

The objective of this section is to examine the various study methods that we have used so far commonly in our practice and the efficacy of such methods. We need to learn the methods that will address the problem of the forgetting curve. To put it succinctly, you will examine the methods and then figure out the best ways to learn the new information by the end of this chapter.

Thankfully, we don't need to start from scratch to assess the various methods of learning. Psychologist John Dunlosky from Kent State University has already conducted decades of research on different learning techniques to examine the efficacy of the various techniques. He and his team of researchers finally concluded that effectively there are ten learning methodologies[3]. Few of them are commonly used, but they are not effective. However, few others are very effective, but are rarely used.

Here are the ten learning techniques examined by Dunlosky for testing their effectiveness:

1. Re-Reading
2. Highlighting and underlining
3. Summarization
4. Keyword mnemonics
5. Imagery for text.
6. Practice Testing
7. Distributed Practice
8. Interleaved practice
9. Elaborative Interrogation
10. Self-Explanation

Besides the ten methods above, Dunlosky's team also looked at some computer-driven

---

[3]https://www.aft.org/sites/default/files/periodicals/dunlosky.pdf

tutors and other technologies that showed some promise in effective learning. Since these technologies can't be made uniformly available to all the students due to cost constraints though, these were excluded from the scope of their study.

Dunlosky and his team's research revealed some surprising facts about the effectiveness of different methods of learning. It shows that the methods that are most commonly used for learning are not the most effective ways of learning. Yet there are some not so commonly used learning methods, that have proven to deliver good results.

Dunlosky in his report has divided the ten methods in three different categories as explained below:

A. Methods Commonly Used In Learning But Ineffective For Long Term Retention.

There are five commonly used methods in our education system or we generally use them when we read something for gaining knowledge, but these are not very effective for learning. Let's summarize each of these methods:

Re-Reading

This method involves just reading the same piece of information over and over again with the assumption that more consumption would equal to more retention.

A survey[4] conducted at one renowned university revealed that a whopping 84% of the students used re-reading and highlighting (see next method) as a method of learning. You can realize that these two strategies are most popular amongst students, probably because it is the easiest thing to do.

Research indicated that (A) re-reading helps with higher-level processing only (reproducing the main ideas) rather than details, and (B) the beneficial effects are greater if the rereading is "spaced"—that is, it occurs a week or two after the initial reading. Also, re-reading doesn't always enhance the understanding of the subject, and also its benefits are not long-lasting, as

---

[4] https://www.ncbi.nlm.nih.gov/pubmed/19358016

compared to the other methods, that you will learn later in this section.

Highlighting

Highlighting involves students marking what they consider to be important parts of the material while reading by underlining or using a colored marker. Active highlighting helps student performance more than passive highlighting (someone else has highlighted what the student is reading). This probably indicates that actively choosing what is important involves extra mental processing that is beneficial. The less text highlighted the better. The quality of the highlighting matters—meaning that students first actively assessed the importance of information and then only highlighted rather than just read and highlighted every second sentence of the textbook.

Highlighting may appear to be effective, because you apply additional emphasis on the highlighted portion, but there is a study that showed that highlighting as a method of learning didn't help. Rather, it was counter-productive. The study showed[5] that the group of students who highlighted the text and then revised the text at a later stage performed the worst in terms of recalling the information as compared to the other group, who reviewed the clean text. Dunlosky concluded that highlighting is merely a starting point of learning, and therefore needs to be accompanied by more effective studying methods.

Summarization

In this learning technique, the students are required to summarize what they have learned about a subject. The central point of this technique is that you should be able to write down in shortest form the central idea of the information you just learned while disregarding the unimportant information. Though this technique is useful, the limitation of this technique is that it requires teaching the students how to summarize to enhance learning and retention. One study showed that the students who were given the required coaching on the best ways to summarize the

5

https://www.tandfonline.com/doi/abs/10.1080/193880 79209558078?journalCode=ulri19 reading material were able to recall the information as compared to the others who were not given the coaching.

Therefore, the extensive training requirement under this approach makes this method less feasible. This extensive training requirement to develop summarization skills would in itself make it a new subject. So the teachers who already feel overwhelmed with the learning material would be least motivated to adopt this learning method. Moreover, the younger students may find it difficult to write high quality summaries and therefore not get the full benefit by this method.

Keyword Mnemonics

Do you remember the way kids are taught to learn the types of stars by remembering "Oh Be A Fine Girl/Guy, Kiss Me"? Here, the first letter of each word indicates the type of star in the sky. For example, O is for O class stars—the hottest ones, B stands for B Class stars—the blueish ones. These are called **keyword mnemonics**.

The benefit of mnemonics is that you remember some easy-to-remember keywords as a sentence that supports your ability to remember the otherwise difficult information. The more interesting you make the keywords, the better are your chances of remembering them (kissing a girl or guy is obviously an interesting one and easy to remember).

Similarly, I recall using VIBGYOR as a keyword mnemonics to remember the different colors of a rainbow, namely violet, indigo, blue, green, yellow, orange, and red.

But this method has a limitation, because you can't have mnemonics for everything you need to learn. It also requires dedicating specific time for different concepts to be learned. If given a huge amount of learning material, it would not be feasible to develop mnemonics for everything.

Imagery for Text

There is another way similar to the previous method in which the learner uses imagery to remember particular information or details. For example, if you have to recollect a cockroach bigger than

36

the size of elephant to highlight the diseases that a cockroach can cause by spreading the germs from unhygienic places to your house, it will be an imagery for learning about the precautions to be taken against the diseases that can spread due to cockroaches. Our right brains understands imagery better, just as our left brains loves logic, so the use of imagery may help both sides of the brain.

Research has shown that the benefits of imagery are short-lived. This strategy is not feasible to be used widely. Younger students may find difficulty in acquiring images for complex learning material. Moreover, most of the content to be learned in the school is not image-friendly.

B. Learning Strategies Proven To Be Effective

As you read above and probably have experienced already, a few of the above methods are popular but not very effective as per Dunlosky's research. They are often used because they are easy, but their efficacy in building long term learning and memory is proven by research to be not very effective. As the learning methods listed above are not effective, it is not worth spending any more time on them. Now let's talk about the other spectrum of Dunlosky's study to understand the other strategies for learning effectively.

Practice Testing

Building muscles requires you to stress them out by exercising. Long term learning is not very different. Your brain is also a muscle and therefore, it also needs challenges for its growth. Practice testing is something that works as a stress for your brain muscles, and therefore it is useful for long term retention of information.

Practice testing means formative assessment (procedures conducted by teachers during the learning process in order to modify teaching and learning activities to improve student retention) typically done outside of class and for which students receive at least right-wrong feedback (ideally guided feedback about what they did wrong, but often they are left to figure this out on their own or from peers). It includes any kind of testing students engage in on their own, including (but not limited to) actual or virtual flashcards, practice problems, questions at the end of textbook chapters, and online practice tests and supporting materials provided by textbook publishers.

Practically speaking, unless we are forced to take some exam, we don't offer ourselves to test our retention of information that we learned over a period of time. Once we are out of college or finished with our academic or professional qualifications, we rarely subject ourselves to any testing. But Dunlosky suggests this approach as one of the best learning techniques for deepening our knowledge about any subject.

Most people wouldn't wish to put themselves in the situation of examination again after they have come out of formal education. Obviously, nobody wants to go through those phases of anxiety and stress due to high stakes involved in examinations. But limiting the scope of practice testing to only formal examinations is such a limited application of this great learning strategy, researchers say.

One study conducted at University of Illinois in 1909 and many studies thereafter showed that if students are required to use their memory recall skills after learning, that gives much better results than by merely re-reading or highlighting text.

If a student simply keeps on reading something again and again, this is not going to yield much better results. However, if the student after reading something hides the learning material portion with his hand, and tries to recall the same information from his or her memory, this will positively boost long term learning.

The use of the practice test technique before a final examination does the job of retrieval of information. Merely feeding the information in your head by re-reading is not an active utilization of your brain's faculties. Getting your brain to work by recalling the information that you just consumed is something that is called **active participation** in learning. The information learned through recalling from memory deepens the learning.

The use of flashcards in learning is one of the ways to do practice testing. The flashcard showing all the questions on the front and the right answer on the back of it can be used for practice testing. The idea here is that until you can recall the information required to answer the question stated on the flashcard, you will have to put the flashcard back in the stack. Only once you have recalled the information from your memory, the flashcard can leave the stack.

Another way to strengthen the practice testing approach is to develop the right habit of note-taking. While learning, you must take appropriate notes. You may also assign different symbols for different ideas in your notes. Just to give you a personal example of the usage of different symbols, I used to put symbols like "$" in the margins of my textbooks for concepts talking about the differences between two things or a triangle or a star to refer to different ideas in the notes. Appropriate ways of note-taking helps during your practice test or memory recall process by providing additional support to form new learning neural pathways for storage of the information. We have a complete section on note-taking later in the book that will help you understand the best ways to learn.

Distributed Practice

The most popular way to study is studying everything together in one long stretch before your exam or test. Students generally spend one full night reading or refreshing all the information in one sitting. This process is known as **massed practice**, because you have dedicated a longer time period for studying something. The other approach is to dedicate lesser amount of time every evening spread over a few days prior to the examination, which time would be equivalent to the total amount being spent in one sitting. This approach is called **distributed practice** of learning. It is is about spreading practice or study activities over time, rather than cramming near the exam deadline.

Let's try to understand distributed practice by one example. Take a simple example of a first-grader who is preparing for a spelling test. Now, there could be two approaches to it. One, she reads the spelling of the single word and practices to learn the spelling by writing the spelling of this word several times below that word. After that, she moves on to the next word and then practices writing that word several times again. She follows this approach to remember the spelling of many words by this approach. The student here is following a massed practice. There is another approach for preparing for this spelling test as well. Now, the student will read the spelling of a word, write this under the word, and then immediately move to reading the spelling of a next word and practice that. She goes on to do that until she finishes all the words. After that, she would again follow the entire sequence of writing say twenty words several times in a row. This practice will distribute the learning process with a gap of nineteen more words before she practice the same word again. Here, she is following the approach of distributed practice.

The irony is that students prefer learning by way of massed practice because of a few reasons. One, it saves them from investing time every day for longer time spans, and it requires enough motivation and exercise of self-discipline to do that. Secondly, massed practice in one sitting makes you feel confident in that you will remember the information stored in your memory for the immediate purpose of taking the exam the next morning, though it is proven that this strategy fails beyond passing the exam, and doesn't help to retain long term learning.

The research has proved that students retain knowledge and skills for comparatively a longer period of time if they follow the distributed practices approach instead of massed practice. Distributed practice may take comparatively more effort and longer time as compared to the massed practice.

Dunlosky gives some examples where we are not conscious of following the distributed practice approach to ensure longer term learning. For example, if you wish to learn dancing, you don't do massed practice i.e., you don't practice all types of dancing steps in one go, rather you practice for many days or weeks to learn different dancing steps every evening. However, you don't follow this dance learning analogy in preparation for the examination. Because most students try to defer the studying until a day before the examination, and when you come to know that tomorrow is examination, then there is no other option left except cramming. There is no scope of distributed practice, because it requires prior planning and self-discipline to do the distributed practice.

Distributed practice requires forming the right set of habits and exercise of enough self-discipline on the part of the learner. I have written another book entitled _The Power of Self Discipline_, which you might find useful if you are willing to learn effective techniques for developing self discipline for implementation of learning techniques.

C. Learning Strategies Without Enough Evidence But Still Showing Strong Promises:

Interleaved practice:

This method of learning is a next-level approach as compared to the distributed practice. **Interleaved Practice** involves mixing different kinds of problems or study material within a single study session. The conventional approach is to learn all aspects of one concept, solve practice problems or activities applying that concept, and then move on to the next one in a linear fashion. Under this approach also, similar to the distributed practice, you don't do the repetition of one particular concept in massed manner, rather you put the gaps in a way that after practicing one type of learning material, you switch to another type of learning material for practicing.

Therefore, the broader learning approach under interleaved practice is similar to the distributed practice. However, there is one key difference: While in distributed practice you practice different concepts in a row, but the topic of different material is similar in nature, in interleaved practice, you choose altogether different material for practicing.

Take an example of the subject of mathematics. In the massed practice approach, the students will pick up the addition-related problems and practice them in a row, and then they move to subtraction, multiplication, or division problems. However, in interleaved practice, the students will practice one question of addition-related problems, then they will pick subtraction as the next problem, then multiplication, and so on. Interleaved practice will involve solving one problem for each type (i.e. addition, subtraction, multiplication, and division) before solving a new problem for each type.

In a 2006 study[6], Doug Rohrer and Kelli Taylor, researchers from University of South Florida, experimented to measure the efficacy of interleaved practice versus massed practice. In the experiment, students were required to undergo two practice tests before they could go to the final examination. The students were divided in two different groups. One group was asked to solve the problem related to one type of solid (say a wedge), and they were given four different version of the same type of solid for practicing. Then they were given a different type of problem, for which they had to solve four versions of the problem. You'd have already guessed that this was the example of massed practice.

The another set of students was given the problems in a shuffled manner i.e. they solved one problem for finding area of a wedge, then the next problem was related to computing the area of a spherical

---

[6] https://files.eric.ed.gov/fulltext/ED505642.pdf

cylinder, and then some other type of the problem. In a way, they never practice the same type of problem in a row, unlike the first group of students. This is an example of interleaved practice.

After the practice tests were done and the final exams were over, the result of the experiment was checked. It was noted that the first set of students did far better than the second group in the initial practice test. But the result of the final examination (that was conducted later) was much different. The students who did interleaved practice fared three time better than the students who did massed practice.

Similarly, the positive effects of interleaving practice were also tested in the realm of sports. In one study[7] conducted, college basketball players were asked to practice three different types of pitches. One group of students was doing the practices in a massed practice manner i.e. practicing the same pitch over and over before moving to the next type. Another group was told to

---

[7]

http://citeseerx.ist.psu.edu/viewdoc/download?doi=10.1.1.172.8751&rep=rep1&type=pdf

practice in an interleaved manner i.e. practicing different pitches one after the other. The results showed that the students who had practiced in interleaved manner had a better hitting performance as compared to the other group.

However, as compared to the strategies of practice testing and the distributed practice (as covered in category B above), Dunlosky candidly stated that the interleaved practice strategy was not researched quite enough to show more evidence (unlike practice testing and distributed practice). But that doesn't mean that this strategy lacks the effectiveness in learning; it only lacks enough research evidence. Despite lack of enough research, as per Dunlosky, this strategy of learning is quite a promising strategy to implement.

Elaborative Interrogation

The next approach, as was tested in the research by Dunlosky, is detailed questioning about any subject. This approach involves detailed interrogation about any new subject being learned. The learner is required to generate an explanation for why an explicitly stated fact or concept is true.

For example, assume you are a student of economics and you are being taught about the law of supply and demand, which states that if demand of any product is more than its supply, then the prices will go up. Alternatively, if supply is more, then the prices will go down. Under the elaborative interrogation methodology, the student will do a further interrogation about the rationale behind this law of economics. Now, the student would try to explain why this fact is true. She would test this principle by testing it with some real life situation. The student might think that since less rain is caused by a bad monsoon in a particular year, the grain crops would be less in supply and there would be more people who would need the grains. Since there is shortage, people will be willing to pay more money to get the grain for their household usage. You see, if the student understands the underlying reasons through elaborative interrogation, then she would understand this concept from a long term learning perspective.

Self-Explanation

Under the approach of self-explanation, the student will try to explain how this new piece of information is related to the information she already knows. Like the approach of elaborative interrogation, this self-explanation also takes the form of asking yourself to question yourself. **Self-explanation** involves students to communicate in their own words how new information is related to known information, or explaining steps taken during problem solving. It enhances learning by helping integrate new information with pre-existing knowledge.

For example, if you want to learn about the law of earth's gravity, you would try to ask yourself some questions and then try to answer them. You will ask what will happen if there is no gravity. Then you will realize that this will be a catastrophic situation. You will analyze that earth is simply one big sphere in the universe that rotates around the sun in one solar system, and that there are numerous such solar systems in the world. If there is no gravitational force, then how will the thing remain affixed to the earth? What will hold the water in the big ocean? Then you will realize that if there is no force of gravity, there can't be any life on the earth because no living being will be able to stay on the earth. There will be no living organisms in the sea, as water can't be held by the ocean. This whole self-explanation tells you about the law of gravity from a lifetime learning perspective.

The reason why the strategies above work for longer term retention is because this involves active processing of the content to understand it and assimilate with the prior knowledge of the student.

To conclude, the last three strategies i.e. Interleaved practice, Interrogation, and Self-explanation show enough promise to deliver the results, but due to lack of enough research material to substantiate the effectiveness of them, it could be put at par with the other two proven strategies i.e. Practice Testing and Distributed Practice.

If you are learning as a student to pass certain exams or you are generally learning something new, like a new language or a music skill, etc. you better have researched learning strategies now that you can put them to use.

Now let's move to the next chapter, where we will explore some more learning techniques that can be used in any area of life apart from studying.

Chapter 4: Few Key Nuances You Should Know About Learning

****

"Learning is not attained by chance, it must be sought for with ardor and diligence." ~ Abigail Adams

Real Knowledge vs. Pretend Knowledge

Each of us is striving to learn the best possible ways that serves to improve our lives. Our objective is to gain deep real knowledge, and not merely surface-level knowledge. After all, the objective of learning anything new is to imbibe the new knowledge deeply within our brains and to transform that into our personal wisdom—that in turn helps us to make better decisions. And ultimately, seemingly small decisions impact the quality of your life. The quality of your life depends on the quality of decisions you choose to make. As Tony Robbins once rightly said, "It is in your moments of decision that your destiny is shaped."

Therefore how to make better decisions boils down to gaining real knowledge and not merely gaining surface-level information. The objective of gaining knowledge shouldn't be to show off your use of heavy jargon. Rather, you want to gain real and deep knowledge to help you take better decisions in your life.

I recently came across something interesting about the difference between real knowledge versus pretend knowledge, and a story told by Charlie Munger, the billionaire partner of Warren Buffett (at a commencement to USC Law School in 2007) explains this difference very well in below words.

> I frequently tell the apocryphal story about how Max Planck, after he won the Nobel Prize, went around Germany giving the same standard lecture on the new quantum mechanics.
>
> Over time, his chauffeur memorized the lecture and said, *"Would you mind, Professor Planck, because it's so boring to stay in our routine, if I*

gave the lecture in Munich and you just sat in front wearing my chauffeur's hat?" Planck said, *"Why not?"* And the chauffeur got up and gave this long lecture on quantum mechanics. After which a physics professor stood up and asked a perfectly ghastly question. The speaker said, *"Well I'm surprised that in an advanced city like Munich I get such an elementary question. I'm going to ask my chauffeur to reply."*

Everyone would be amazed with the presence of mind this chauffeur displayed through his quick-wittedness to handle the situation. But the moot point here is to distinguish between real knowledge and pretend knowledge. This chauffeur didn't make efforts to get the deep and real knowledge, rather it was all pretend knowledge.

Apply Feynman's technique for gaining real knowledge.

Richard Feynman, an American physicist and a Nobel laureate explained the difference between real knowledge and pretend knowledge in the words below:

"In this world we have two kinds of knowledge. One is Planck knowledge, the people who really know. They've paid the dues, they have the aptitude. And then we've got chauffeur knowledge. They've learned the talk. They may have a big head of hair, they may have fine temper in the voice, they'll make a hell of an impression."

Therefore, he devised one simple technique that helps you to gain real knowledge of any subject, instead of merely filling you with some surface level knowledge.

This technique is known as the Feynman technique coined after the name of Richard Feynman (it is also one of the _mental models_), which helps you develop an in-depth understanding of any concept. This approach is a targeted learning approach.

Here are the *four steps* of Feynman Technique:

Step 1: Identify the concept

Take a sheet of paper and write the name of the concept that you want to learn at the top of that page.

Step 2: Explain in plain language

Now, start explaining the concept in your own words as if you were asked to teach it to someone else. The most important thing to remember here is **not to use the technical jargon** that you have read in your learning material. You have to explain the concept in plain, simple language.

Many people tend to use jargon or terminology of the subject in their explanation to others, even when they don't understand the concept very clearly. This is because using jargon conceals our misunderstanding from the people around us. Therefore, don't cheat yourself. The approach should be to use plain and simple language, as if you are teaching the concept to your 70-year-old grandmother, who has no knowledge about the concept.

Step 3: Review the Gap

In this step, you need to review your explanation honestly. Here, you will identify the areas where you didn't know something completely or where you feel your explanation was wavering or not clear. Here, you have to stop, and go back to the learning material, or previous notes prepared for learning the concept.

Step 4: Re-organize and Summarize

Once you have clearly understood the missing concepts, then you need to again explain those concepts in plain language. If there are still any areas in your explanation where you've used jargon, subject terminology or complex language, challenge yourself to re-write these sections in simpler terms. Make sure your explanation could be understood by someone without the knowledge base you believe you already have.

Therefore this Feynman technique will help you learn anything faster by honestly identifying gaps in your understanding of any concept. The Feynman Technique is useful for learning a new idea, understanding an existing idea better, or preparing yourself for discussions on any complex topic.

Let's move further now and talk about some more approaches to learning better.

Learning By Applying the 80:20 Principle

Vilfredo Pareto developed the 80:20 principle in 1906 and it is also known as Pareto's Principle. The principle states that the world works on the rule that only 20% of your activities (even lesser) deliver 80% results (even more) in your life. It could be substantiated by following facts:

1. 99% of the **world's wealth** is accumulated by only 1% of the people.
2. 80% or more of every **business's turnover/profits** are contributed by only 20% or fewer of its customers.
3. If you **satisfy 20% of the people** in your life with your work, that will give you an 80% assurance of the perfect working life.

This rule is applied in so many fields and in its simplest form, basically states that you get 80% of the results from 20% of the work. The percentage under this rule is not abstract and it cannot be applied in absolute terms in every field, but the principle remains that a very small percentage of things attribute to a substantial percentage of results.

In learning any new language also, the concept of 80:20 exists. In any language, it is a small percentage of vocabulary that serves most of the comprehension and understanding requirement for that language.

Tim Ferriss in one of his book states that:

- *95% proficiency with conversational Spanish = 2,500 words = You can learn in 5 months.*

- *98% proficiency with conversational Spanish = 100,000 words = You will take 5 years to learn.*

It means that just 2,500 words that is just 2.5% of even not the complete Spanish language, gives you 95% proficiency in speaking. And you can achieve this massive proficiency in just 5 months of practice.

If you just want 80% proficiency, maybe 2 to 3 months learning is sufficient. But Tim Ferriss states that the real trick is finding that 2.5% of any specific language.

If you are more serious about learning a particular language, you need to follow Benny Lewis, who was interviewed by Tim Ferriss. Benny Lewis, founder of a blog "Fluent in 3 Months" and who speaks multiple languages like Spanish, French, German, Italian, Dutch to list a few, has explained his way of learning multiple language in this interesting TED Talk[8] .

Do watch this video as this guy is hilarious when he speaks so many different languages with such an ease. He explains the principles how he has learned so many languages following the principles of 80:20 by focusing on the most important vocabulary of any language to learn any new language.

Moreover, not only language, but any aspect of learning involves 80:20 principle. In my practice of corporate law in past, it was not that the whole corporate law

[8] https://www.fluentin3months.com/tedx/

statute matter, rather it was only limited number of provisions that are considered most important from any merger, acquisition, or investment deal's perspective. The acquiring entity is most concerned about the legal provisions related to acquiring controlling stake, exercising of voting powers in key business decisions, the right to terminate and exit out of the contract in the event of default or happening of certain contingencies. As a lawyer, if one has mastered the skill in relation to those limited provisions (at a deeper level), he or she would be in a position to handle any complex transaction with even lesser knowledge on the other aspects of the corporate transactions, thanks to the applicability of 80:20 principle here.

Whatever area of learning you may choose; if you want to progress faster in that area, put your energy and efforts in learning the key 20% part of the skill which gives you 80% of the results. This will help you to see results faster, and you will feel motivated to learn the skills faster.

Now, let's understand how our learning is done through association of connected information and in isolation in the next approach based on human psychology.

Associative Learning Approach

Let's do a quick experiment to understand the concept of associative learning. Sit back and close your eyes. Relax and you have to get ready to recall some specific details. Imagine your fathers' right eyebrow. Not his left eyebrow. Not his eyes. Not his forehead . Just his left eyebrow. You must be finding it hard to just recall only one specific body part. When you try to envision your father's eyebrow, you see his eyes, cheeks, forehead, nose, chin—his whole face! Why is it so difficult to recall just his eyebrow?

Associative learning is a learning principle that states that ideas and experiences reinforce each other and can be mentally linked to one another. In a nutshell, it means our brains were not designed to recall information in isolation; instead, we group information together into one associative memory. Associative learning is a theory that states that ideas reinforce each other and can be linked to one another. That's why it is difficult to recall just one eyebrow without seeing the whole face.

Associative learning can be a powerful classroom management and teaching tool. It can be used to help students connect with information more deeply and recall that information.

There are two key types of associative learning: **classical conditioning**, such as in Pavlov's dog (explained below); and **operant conditioning**, or the use of reinforcement through rewards and punishments.

a. Classical Conditioning (stimuli vs. response)

Classical conditioning is a concept based on the premise that learning occurs when you learn something based on a new stimulus. The most famous example is by a Russian psychologist Ivan Pavlov's use of dogs to demonstrate that a stimulus, such as the ringing of a bell, leads to a reward, or food. It involves the use of a stimulus—such as the bell in Pavlov's experiments with the dogs—that is paired with a reward, resulting in salivation by the dogs in the expectation of receiving food.

Here is how it started. The people who fed Pavlov's dogs wore lab coats. Pavlov noticed that the dogs began to drool whenever they saw lab coats, even if there was no food in sight. Pavlov wondered why the dogs salivated at lab coats and not just at food. Then Pavlov thought to conduct this experiment with the dogs. He, in the first step, fed his dogs with meat powder, which naturally made the dogs salivate—salivating is a reflexive response to the meat powder. At this stage, meat powder is the unconditioned stimulus (US) and the salivation is the unconditioned response (UR).

The experiment went on further with a slight change in approach. Now Pavlov rang a bell before presenting the meat powder. The first time Pavlov rang the bell, the neutral stimulus, the dogs did not salivate, but once he put the meat powder in their mouths they began to salivate. After numerous pairings of bell and food, the dogs learned that the bell signalled that food was about to come and began to salivate when they heard the bell. Once this occurred, the bell became the conditioned stimulus (CS) and the salivation to the bell became the conditioned response (CR).

Over repeated trials, the **conditioned stimulus causes learning**. On the other hand, repeated number of instances without offering the reward leads to extinction of the behavior. When the conditioned stimulus, the ringing of the bell, happens before the reward, the person or the animal has time to figure out that the bell ringing means something and learn or form an association.

Not merely on animals, later on this classical conditioning experiment was also done on humans too by two scientists namely JB Watson and Rayner, though it was somewhat unethical. A nine-month old boy Albert was tested for this experiment. He was shown a white rat at some intervals, but every time the rat was shown to him, they made a loud sound along with it. With that, Albert got frightened upon the sight of white rat, as he started to associated the white rat with loud noise, even if at later times, there was no loud noise made upon showing the white rat. The experiment was known as Little Albert's Experiment proved the relevance of associative learning amongst humans as well.

b. Operant Conditioning (negative reinforcement)

Another form of associative learning was experimented by psychologist B.F. Skinner known as operant conditioning. This concept involves the use of a schedule of reinforcements, or rewards and punishments, until the behavior is learned.

For instance, if the dog were to hear the bell and step on a lever, it would receive the dog biscuit, the reward. Alternatively, if the dog were to step on the lever when the bell doesn't ring and receive a shock—a **positive punishment**—that would shape a behavior in the opposite direction. A **negative punishment**, by contrast, would be to take away something, such as a biscuit, if the dog barks.

There are several differences between classical and operant conditioning. While the basic feature of operant conditioning is reinforcement, classical conditioning relies more on association between stimuli and responses. A second distinction is that much of operant conditioning is based on voluntary behavior, while classical conditioning often involves involuntary reflexive behavior.

By using these principles, you can associate your learning with some stimuli or induce some reinforcement by way of punishments. For example, impressing your friend with your new language skills can be a real stimulant for you to learn better. Now, you know that if you learn better, you get a reward–to impress him or her, or to get the chance to spend time with him or her to teach something that you learned.

Take another example. Your boss or your teacher happens to behave very badly if you reach your office or school late even by a minute. Now, to avoid spoiling your day with bad behavior, you would train your mind to reach the place ten minutes before (also taking into account the traffic or other exigencies that might come in the way).

Learn Anything in 20 Hours

I was quite intrigued when I first listened to Josh Kaufman, author of *The First 20 Hours: How to Learn Anything Fast,* in his TED Talk[9] about how you can learn anything in twenty hours. In this world, where we have concepts like the 10,000 hour rule to become an expert in any skill, this message of learning anything in 20 hours seemed quite provocative to me in the first instance. Therefore I was curious to understand this concept better.

But to my utmost surprise, what I learned about the concept was quite practical. Josh explained that there is a difference between becoming an expert in something vs. becoming good in something. Expert means touching the top level in one's field, whereas being reasonably good at something means you can handle that activity reasonably well. The idea is to learn enough that transforms you from **'being grossly incompetent'** to **'reasonably good at something.'**

---

[9] https://www.youtube.com/watch?v=5MgBikgcWnY

Take an example: learning only a few important elements of a foreign language doesn't make you an expert; but it can make you reasonably good at the language. And with such knowledge, you can manage to stay in that country and have reasonable conversations with the people around in the foreign land—meaning you learned in a way that practically serves your purpose (by the way, you will see more information about how to learn the different languages in a shortest time later in this section).

Therefore, if your goal is to have a reasonable understanding of some field, and you don't have any intention of becoming an expert in that field, you can achieve your learning goal in 20 hours. Here are the important elements of this 20-hour roadmap to learning something new.

Step 1: Deconstruct the skill.

To learn any new skill, the first step is to break that skill into various small components. Remember every big skill is a bundle of many small skills covered in it. Now, once you have deconstructed the skill, the important thing to remember is to practice the most important parts of that skill first. The main thing here is to practice intelligently; given our objective of becoming reasonably good at something in fewer than 20 hours. Therefore, while deconstructing, you have to identify the most important sub-skills needed that will give you maximum advantage – you need to follow 80:20 principle.

To give you an example of my self-publishing business, this involves quite a few skills. If someone were to look at it as a whole, it will seem onerous to even think of taking it up. This book publishing business is not just a process of writing; it has various other components involved. You have to have technical skills for uploading the book, you need to creatively get the cover designs finalized. It doesn't stop there, you need to develop online marketing skills and network with other content creators.

Now to gain advantage through authorship, though, the most important skill to develop is to write something, but you have to learn all other skills before you can generate a self-published bestseller book. Therefore, the first step is to deconstruct the skill into various sub-skills and then you have to choose the most important sub-skills and spend more time in practicing that.

Step 2: Learn Just Enough

When you are starting out to learn any mini-skill (as a subset of the major skill), you don't need to become an expert before you start out. Rather, you need to learn just enough, so that when you find yourself committing mistakes, you can self-correct yourself.

To continue the previous example of self-publishing business, I started writing without books without any formal coaching, rather I just bought one of the best books on the subject about how to write and promote books on Kindle from one of the self-publishing industry veterans namely author Steve Scott. I just learned enough and then started writing my first book. This bare minimum but quality learning helped me to write my first book. I didn't wait to write until I became expert. I just learned enough so I could start. I precisely acted on the principle recommended by Jim Rohn, who said: *"You don't need to be great to start; You need to start to be great."*

Step 3: Remove Barriers to practice.

The next step in the process is to remove any obstacles that may come as a hindrance to your practicing of the sub-skill. Generally, TV is the biggest culprit, followed by our smartphones that steal our willpower as we drift away from practicing. Learning anything new for the first time definitely brings some frustration; you don't feel like progressing faster in your chosen domain. There you have to safeguard yourself from any distractions so you remain focused on your journey towards learning the skill.

Step 4: Practice for 20 hours.

You are now set with your list of mini activities or sub-skills to be done and also taken care of removing the barriers to the practice. Now, you need to practice this for 20 hours.

Here is something important. You don't have to practice for twenty hours in one stretch. As you learned the distributed practice learning method, this approach follows that principle. Also, it is not humanly possible to practice all in one stretch due to human attention span limitations.

20 hours of practice would roughly mean 45 minutes of practice for a period of *thirty* days in a row. And that's achievable.

This practice of 45 minutes daily builds in it the concept of spaced repetition through interleaved practice principle; as you would be doing all other things everyday and then loop in the practicing of this particular skill for 45 minutes every day.

The four steps above, if followed well, can help you become reasonably good in anything you want to learn, be it a new language, be it playing guitar, learning martial arts, or any other skill. In fact, the major barrier in learning anything new is not intellectual, rather it is emotional. We often get scared of sounding stupid, if we are learning something new and miss out few things. And that fear of sounding stupid often stops us from trying anything new; whereas in reality, you can learn anything if you really wish to.

Again, taking a personal example, when I published my first book along with my full-time day job, I remember writing every evening for around 30 minutes to one hour after my office hours. This daily practice of writing 1,000 words every evening gave me a reward of a 25,000-word book in a period of 5 to 6 weeks—from start to end, edited with cover design and ready to publish. That's the power of repeated practice.

I know 20 hours to learn anything new seems very little, but this approach of spreading 20 hours in 30 even days is based on the principles on which our brain's neural network and memory works, as evidenced by the studies on distributed practice and interleaved practice. As stated earlier, this approach doesn't target to make you an expert (which we will cover in the later section of the book), but you will get rid of your false inner excuses and get comfortable with trying anything new, be it learning some musical instrument or practicing any foreign language or any other thing.

Now, let's move to the next section of the book to talk about different learning styles and interesting findings about the concept.

Chapter 5: What is Your Learning Style and Myths About It?

****

"Tell me and I forget, teach me and I may remember, involve me and I learn." — Benjamin Franklin

Different Learning Styles

You must have already read about the articles explaining about everyone having a different preference of learning something new. It is said that some people learn by reading the material, but some like to learn by watching it. Then some people say that they are more of a listener, while few others would say that they learn by better by practically doing it by their hands.

The proponents of different learning-style theory have different version of learning styles. Most people say there are three styles, namely auditory, visual, and physical. There are some others that say there are more. Even there is no consensus in the number of such methods. But it is more often referred that there are **seven different learning styles**. Some people may find one style as their dominant style of learning with far less use of other styles. Some people use mixed styles for learning. There is no right or wrong style, and also no one has a fixed learning style for life that can't be changed.

But why is this idea of different learning styles so popular in the first place?

It is because parents tend to think that their children are being taught an education specific to their kid's learning style. Similarly, teachers also start to believe that they are more sensible towards the needs of the children to help them learn in the best possible way, as most suitable to them.

Now there are different schools of thoughts about the efficacy of different styles in the process of learning. We will come to that, but before that let's have a quick look at these various styles and what does it mean to learn by a specific style.

There are seven different learning styles as stated below:

- **Visual (spatial, optical)**

In this style, you prefer using pictures, images, and spatial understanding.

- **Aural (auditory   senses, musical)**:

Aural style means sound and music is your preferred way of learning in this style.

- **Verbal (linguistic)**:

You like to learn primarily by using words, both in speech and writing, if you have verbal learning style.

- **Physical (kinesthetic)**:

Under this style, you prefer to learn by using your body, hands, and sense of touch.

- **Logical (mathematical)**:

Using logic, reasoning, pattern detection, and systems are the main drivers for learning in this style. You learn by way of idea diagrams, process maps, etc.

- **Social (interpersonal)**:

This is generally a preferred way for people who are extroverted in nature. Here, you enjoy learning in groups or with other people. You learn best when brainstorming with others, bouncing ideas of each other, proposing and polishing ideas—you need others to give you feedback.

- **Solitary (intrapersonal)**:

For those loving solitude and enjoy their own company, this is their preferred mode of learning. Here, you prefer to work alone and use self-study.

Brain Parts and Learning Style

There is something unique about this learning style. Brain science has found that each learning style uses different parts of the brain. Researchers using brain-imaging technologies have been able to find out the key areas of the brain responsible for each learning style. You will understand this better by looking at the image and the explanation below:

- **Visual:** The occipital lobes at the back of the brain manages the visual sense. Both the occipital and parietal lobes manage spatial orientation.

- **Aural:** The temporal lobes handle aural content. The right temporal lobe is especially important for music.

- **Verbal:** The <u>temporal and frontal lobes,</u> especially two specialized regions called Broca's and Wernickeï's areas (in the left hemisphere of these two lobes), are responsible for verbal style of learning.

- **Physical:** The <u>cerebellum and the motor cortex</u> (at the back of the frontal lobe) handle much of our physical movement.

- **Logical:** The <u>parietal lobes</u>, especially the left side, drive our logical thinking.

- **Social:** The <u>frontal and temporal lobes</u> handle much of our social activities.

- **Solitary:** The <u>frontal and parietal lobes, and the limbic system</u>, are also active with this style.

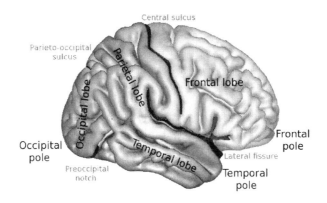

Of course, you may say that you love a particular way of learning as compared to others. I personally think that reading i.e. verbal, and listening are my most preferred ways of learning. I don't feel like learning through visuals or videos much—maybe due to the reasons that you have to be stationed at one place while watching videos, as compared to listening that you can do while moving around places, walking, jogging, exercising, or even washing dishes. Yes, everyone has different preferences for learning.

Now, let's come to the question:

Is there any scientific evidence that distinguishes that any particular method is more effective compared to other methods?

Answer is no. There is no research out there that shows that one method of learning is superior than another.

Christian Jarret, a cognitive neuroscientist, states that there is a very little evidence about the efficacy of the different learning style. Whatever evidence is out there is very weak to justify usage of any specific method for learning. Convincing evidence for learning styles would show that people who preferred one learning style learned better when taught material in their favored way, whereas a different group with a different preference learned the same material better when taught in their favored fashion. A study[10] conducted on few students to test the efficacy of learning based on their learning style proved that there was no strong support that verbal learners and visual learners should be given different types of learning material.

Jarret stated that usually **learning anything depends more on the type of learning material instead of learners'**

---

[10]

https://www.sciencedirect.com/science/article/pii/S1041608006000331

preferred style of learning. The nature of learning material determines the learning style primarily. For example, if you have to learn French, learning it pictorially cannot obviously be the preferred way. Similarly, if you want to learn geometry, it is not possible to learn it verbally—you have to come to the board to do it visually.

If above is true, then is the learning style a total myth?

Leading experts in the field state that the myth of different learning system is not merely a small misconception, rather it is causing harm to the students. The experts say that believing in different learning styles would prompt the teachers to teach the students as per their strengths, but this approach will not address the shortcomings of students. To put it simply, not prompting a student to learn by reading the material, because the student thinks that he learns by better by visual or video, would reduce the learning ability of student by reading.

Professor Stephen Dinham from the Melbourne Graduate School of Education summarizes the danger of teaching to this myth in his recent book *Leading, Teaching, and Learning*:

> "However, it does matter, because of the problems and harm that can be caused by the categorisation, labelling and limiting of learning experiences of students through the continued belief in and application of so-called learning styles. Would we tolerate doctors continuing to use a disproved, harmful treatment?"

The danger of assuming the learning style preference theory is that by labelling students as a certain type of learner and changing the teaching style to match this type of learning, we, as parents or teachers, wrongly encourage students to develop a fixed mindset. A fixed mindset can be thought of as one in which a student's belief of what they can achieve is controlled by their inherited characteristics (for example, predispositions and intelligence) rather than the belief that effort can and does make a difference. Rather students need to be encouraged to think that they can learn in any specific way, if they put their efforts to that.

Also, imparting or designing education specific to different learning styles doesn't make economic sense either, because certain learning styles study materials may come with a high cost and therefore not easily accessible to all students.

Learning By Note Taking

Besides different learning styles, probably you'd have also heard about discussions on different note-taking styles for comprehending the information being consumed. The whole objective of spending time on reading, listening, or consuming new information or encoding in any manner has the objective of better comprehension and retention in the memory, to enable you retrieve the information whenever needed.

Most people inadvertently think that they will remember the information in the future also, while learning something new. Do you recall the last time you created a new password for a software or mobile application? Whenever you create some new password, you tend to wrongly assume that you would remember the password later. But, if you don't note the password somewhere in your notebook or in a computer file, it so happens that later you don't recollect even the simplest of your passwords. I admit that learning anything complicated and more detailed is not comparable to simply remembering a few digits of a password, but the idea here is to impress upon you the need for creating effective tools for later retrieval when you need it most.

It is relevant to mention here that the role of note-taking is not merely limited to memory retention purposes; rather it also helps you to better comprehend the targeted learning material. Better notes help you remember concepts, develop meaningful learning skills, and gain a better understanding of a topic.

For students, effective notes will even lead to less stress when you are near your examinations. Learning how to take better study notes in your classroom sessions helps improve recall and understanding of what you are learning because it:

- Ensures you are actively listening to what the teacher is saying.
- Requires you to think about what you are writing.
- Helps you make connections between topics.
- Serves as quality review material for after class.

Using different note-taking strategies is important, especially as you progress through high school and transition to college or university. There are several note-taking techniques you can use to start taking better notes in class. Everybody has its own preference of selecting the method, so feel free to adopt whatever works better for you.

Cornell Method:

The Cornell Method has been and remains one of the most popular note-taking strategies amongst students. You simply **divide up your notes into 3 sections.**

One containing the keyword or concept, and the other containing the description or notes associated with the keyword or concept. At the bottom of the page, you should write paragraphs summarizing the information contained in the notes.

The right column is home to the **general area.** This is where you keep your most important ideas that the teacher has covered during class. It is important that you try to summarize as much as possible and to be smart when note-taking. On the left hand side, you will note down the keyword or concept that relates to your section of notes.

The last section labelled "summary" should be left blank during class as it is intended for use when you are reviewing and studying the class notes. This reduces the need to keep up with the teacher's delivery and write fast. Here, you try to **develop a short summary** of key points in this section for greater reflection of the class notes.

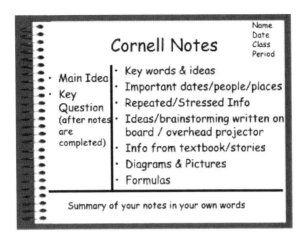

(Image Courtesy: <u>Frank Dauenhauer</u>)

The Cornell method ensures that your notes are neatly organized, summarized, and easy to review later. It allows you to pull major ideas about whatever you learned during your class or important event.

The Mind Mapping Method:

A mind map is a diagram in which ideas, concepts, and images are linked together around a central concept, keyword, or idea.

This method is based on **the use of visual aids** to improve how the brain processes information. It involves using pictures, graphs, diagrams, etc. Rather than writing long paragraphs of information, our brain follows the information sequentially. The use of colours and other visual elements such as different sized letters, also known as **supernotes**, favors the user.

In this method, you generally start with a central idea in the centre of a page. Then you branch out related ideas from the central theme in the form of branches. Each such idea then has further sub-ideas as sub-branches. It is helpful in any complex and lengthy project, where your mind tends to get cluttered with multiple ideas floating in your head and you are not able to put it in orderly manner.

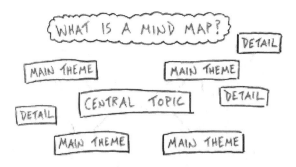

I have implemented and found this idea very useful in writing my books. The theme of the book comes in the centre, then I draw out branches to figure out the different chapters of the book. Thereafter, the next level of arrows emanating from the branches shows the different topics to be covered in each chapter. This approach enables the mind to open up its creativity and to keep generating ideas about what it feels important next to be mentioned here.

In mind mapping, you use both the left and right brains. The left brain is for all logic-related work, and the right brain is involved in the creativity and generation of new ideas.

Now, you can try this out. Take any of your complex learning material that has various components covered in it. Start with the central theme of the subject matter and then draw possible branches of that subject matter, and then keep putting details on each branch. Soon, you will find your complicated subject matter appearing holistically on one sheet in front of you.

Charting Method:

Charting is nothing but a table of rows and columns. The top row normally classifies the concept with descriptions or keywords listed in the row below.

For example, if you have to recall the different theories under psychology or economics, you would make different columns mentioning the name of the theory, the year of publishing, the name of the proposer, and lastly the subject of coverage in that particular theory.

This method enables you to quickly identify facts and their relationships with other information.

The Outlining Method

This method involves writing a series of topics and sub-topics, and identifying them by indenting the text, numbering the lines, or using a dash or bullet point. The outlining note-taking method uses headings and bullet points to organize topics.

The outline method is based on a hierarchy. All ideas are marked with bullet points, nesting corresponding ideas underneath with smaller bullet points.

This method is most useful when learning about topics that include a lot of detail.

Symbols and abbreviation:

No matter which note-taking methods you use, there will be times when you cannot keep pace with the class and your hand and fingers will begin to hurt from writing. Here, the use of symbols and abbreviations becomes very useful for note-taking.

I learned this technique early in my life, while taking notes in class as well as from textbooks. As previously mentioned, I remember that my study books were filled with triangles, stars, circles, and other symbols in the blank spaces of the books. Each symbol had different meaning of my understanding, for example, the "$" was stated for showing difference in two concept, whereas the triangle shape meant that there is an important definition covered in that paragraph of the book. This technique speeds things up, and you can easily memorize these symbols in relation to the concept covered in a particular page.

Flow System:
This approach is a less rigid approach of taking notes. Like mind-mapping, where you prepare circles with arrows for

different kind of interconnected thoughts, this method also requires you to be authentically noting your understanding about what you have learned. The flow system approach was mentioned by Scott Young in his book *Learn More, Study Less*. In this approach, you start by just writing the major ideas of what you have learned. It means you just have to use words instead of long sentences. Though it would mean compromising on readability, it would help you understand the concept better during the lecture.

Once you have written down various ideas, the next step is to connect the ideas with a few arrows. **Instead of capturing idea in an orderly hierarchy, you want to mention the ideas as interrelated concepts**. Connecting the various ideas with arrows clarifies what idea precedes or succeeds the other, or what idea is more important than the others.

Lazy Man's method of note-taking

Under this method, the lecturer or the speaker of the sessions delivers to the attendees the presentation in slides. Thus, when the speaker is explaining the concept to the audience, they already have the printed material with them. The students can refer to the notes while they are listening and can also make additional noting on the slides in the margins. The approach is quite straight forward, and you can't miss any point of the lecture, because the full skeleton of what is being taught in the lecture is with you in advance.

Some speakers or teachers deliver the handouts to the students, but there are lots of blanks in the handouts. The students need to listen the concepts in the lecture to fill in the blanks. This approach forces the students to be attentive or else they won't be able to fill in the blanks. In other words, this method already captures the element of test-taking alongside the delivery of the information.

Now, you have learned about multiple ways of note-taking. You might already knowingly or unconsciously be using some of these techniques for note-taking. The next question that arises is what is the best learning method that you should use for effective learning.

Cornell's method is stated to be widely used method of note-taking, but here you have to prepare a summary for each learning session that may be time consuming. I personally think that the note-taking approach is more of a personal preference of every individual. For me, I used putting abbreviations and symbols as a notes in my earlier days, and currently I use mind-mapping to structure my thoughts around the book. I find these note-taking methods helpful to learn, comprehend, and memorize the information better.

You should also try different styles of note-taking and then stick to the one that suits you best, considering your personal preference and time available to you.

Should You Take Notes By Hand Or At A Computer?

Taking notes on laptops rather than in longhand is increasingly common. Researchers examined the question whether taking notes at computer is better than writing notes by hand.

After studying, many researchers[11] have suggested that laptop note-taking is less effective than longhand note taking for learning. Prior studies have primarily focused on students' capacity for multitasking when using laptops. Further research suggests that even when laptops are used solely to take notes, they may still be impaired learning involved because their use results in shallower processing.

In three studies, the researchers found that students who took notes on laptops performed worse on conceptual questions than students who took notes longhand. The studies show that whereas taking more notes can be beneficial, laptop note-takers' tendency to transcribe lectures verbatim rather than processing information and reframing it in their own words is detrimental to learning.

After reading this research, I tried to implement this approach in my daily morning journal writing. I have been doing morning journaling for many years now.

---

[11]
http://journals.sagepub.com/doi/abs/10.1177/0956797614524581

Earlier, I used to do it in my notebook. Then I shifted to writing in Microsoft Word files on my laptop. But recently, I have again shifted back to the tradition pen and paper approach. I personally feel that when I write down my goals, my areas of learning, and other items in my journal, they stick much longer in my head. I still remember the handwritten notes in my journal from ten years ago, but I don't have a clear memory of what I had typed in my laptop. Though it seemed easy to keep typing on a laptop, when it comes to measuring the effectiveness, handwritten journaling has proven to much better to me.

I follow similar principles for outlining my books. I use the traditional pen and paper (in the form of mind mapping, as explained earlier), and that works pretty well. After a dozen books with multiple bestsellers, I am convinced about the effectiveness of handwritten material. I have shared my personal experience, and you can try to find what suits you better.

The next chapter explains how you can learn effectively by implementing gamification and elements of challenge to speed up your learning process.

Chapter 6: Learning Through Challenges and Games

****

"That is the way to learn the most, that when you are doing something with such enjoyment that you don't notice that the time passes." ~ Albert Einstein

Everyone loves games. If you think games are only for kids, you should consider revisiting your thoughts. We never stop having fun and playing—only the forms change. Games stay with us for our entire lives. A young kid's toy cars turn into formulae 1 racing cars, but the game remains with us.

Albert Einstein indicated that the games are the most elevated form of investigation. He knew games are avenues for something deeper and more meaningful learning. Games promote situational learning or, in other words, learning that occurs in groups of practice during immersive experiences. Oftentimes, playing games is the first method children use to explore higher-order thinking skills associated with creating, evaluating, analyzing, and applying new knowledge.

But how would you make something that is tedious, cumbersome, and a heavy subject so interesting that it becomes fun to learn?

The answer is by introducing the element of gamification in the learning. We all have played long video games, wherein hours would pass by, but we didn't stop. The motivation to score more in the game kept us glued to the gaming screens.

How would you feel if you were told that you can learn anything like a game? Welcome to the world of gamification technology through e-learning.

The **gamification of learning**[12] is an educational approach to motivate students to learn by using a videogame design and game elements in learning environments. The goal is to maximize enjoyment and engagement through

---

12

https://en.wikipedia.org/wiki/Gamification_of_learning

capturing the interest of learners and inspiring them to continue learning.

Wikipedia defines gamification as "the use of game thinking and game mechanics in non-game contexts to engage the people for solving the problems."

It further explains that Gamification, broadly, is a process of defining the elements which comprise games that make those games fun and motivate players to continue playing, and using those same elements in a non-game context to influence behavior. Games applied in learning can be considered as **serious games**, where the learning experience is centred around serious stories. The serious story is "impressive in quality" and "part of a thoughtful process" to achieve learning goals.

One of the examples of gamification is simulation training to teach students to learn to drive a car. Simulation gives the similar experience to the learner as if she is driving on the road itself. The movement of steering, applying brakes, driving the car in the reverse gear, etc., all gives a real-life car driving experience. But the best part is that the learner is not worried about any danger of accident. Simulation training puts the element of game in learning a seemingly tough real-life skill and prepares the learner with enough skills to go on the road with little practice.

Another example of learning through gamification is learning trading into stocks, commodities or currencies, by opening a demo account with the trading and brokerage firms. One of my friends, a finance professional, used this technique to master his learning in currency trading, and he shared his experience with me.

To start learning, he simply opened a demo account with one of the currency trading platforms, which is quite a straight-forward process these days, thanks to multiple online trading apps available to help the new entrants who wish to learn this skill. Now for him, except for investing actual money, every other experience of trading was pretty much in real time environment. He was trading in different currency pairs (e.g. USD vs. GBP or USD vs. Euro, and so on), by applying his knowledge in this gamified version of the real-world trading, but without losing any money as a beginner, which becomes the most common reason for people to quit even before they really start. So this gamification method of learning provided a safe environment for him to brush up his skills and then master it sooner. Now he comfortably trades in the real market with REAL money to win the trades on his side.

Below are some major benefits of learning through gamification:

- It gives a **conducive learning environment**. As noted in the example above, gamification offers you the practical difficulties and the roadblocks that you need to handle, but you do it all in the safe environment. You know in advance that your wrong action or non-action in this situation wouldn't turn into a catastrophic failure. This helps you to apply your intellect in a fearless manner and that enables you to give your best shot.

- It gives a **better learning experience**. If you learn new skills in a fun manner, and if you are deeply engaged in the game, it can significantly enhance your understanding of the new subject.

- Gamification gives you **instant feedback**. You don't have to wait too long to know whether you learned or not, unlike formal examinations. As soon as you finish the game, the scores of your game will teach you where you committed mistakes and thus you are immediately aware about your areas of improvement.

- It **triggers behavior changes**. Every game has multiple levels to cross and it offers various rewards or badges to accomplish those tasks. In these levels, badges are quick motivators to perform better, and missed rewards help you rectify your mistakes. Moreover, the spaced repetition strategies in the gamification do the job of cementing your learning. One more thing, most games now have social collaboration tools, meaning that you can share your progress with your friends and followers. This makes you accountable and once you share, you don't wish to be sounding like a loser, so you keep yourself engaged for longer.

- **Applicable to most of the learning needs**. Gamification can be used to fulfill most learning needs, including induction and onboarding, product sales, customer support, soft skills, awareness creation, and compliance.

You may want to check out one gamification method listed below for enhancing the performance of athletes by giving them challenges.

There is tool called **Strava**, which is probably one of the best gamification methods of learning and prompting athletes to meet the newer challenges of running. Strava is a website and mobile app that is used to track athletic activity via satellite navigation and then uploads and share such activities. Styled as a "Social Network for Athletes," it can be used for a number of sporting activities, but the most popular activities tracked using the software are cycling and running. Record an activity and it goes to your **Strava** feed, where your friends and followers can share their own races and workouts, give kudos to great performances, and leave comments on each other's activities.

Now compare the Strava app learning method with normal running, cycling, or exercising everyday in the morning. You'd have already encountered boredom and a lack of motivation at times. Everybody wants to see a goal or a challenge to be conquered and gamification provides that element to you. If you know that you are performing better than your friends, it boosts your morale; and you gear up to take more challenges, in case you notice that your performance is not up to the mark.

Few other examples of gamification in real life are:

- **Loselt** is a popular weight losing mobile app. The app allows for complete nutrition and calorie counting throughout your day. If you stay within your caloric limits, you are rewarded with a "green" day. Badges can be earned from any activity like simply logging in to losing 10 pounds, making everyone feel accomplished.

- **Duolingo** is another gamification example for learning any new language in a fun, quick, and effective way.

- **Hidrate Spark** is an app that takes care of your hydration. It is developed on the principle that dehydration of your body leads to weight gain. Therefore this app is paired with a smart water bottle to remind you of drinking water. The app keeps on checking your body's water level and if gets low, the bottle starts glowing to remind you to drink water.

Learning By Taking Challenges:

It is not always that you have to involve technology or devise certain system of gamification to promote learning. Oftentimes, merely introducing an element of challenge in your regular work enhances your desire to learn better.

In my corporate world experience, I have few examples where putting an element of challenge and fair competition amongst the different teams in the company has helped improve the learning experience of the team as a whole.

I remember the creation of SGA (small group activities) teams in one of my organizations to promote fair competition amongst the different teams in the organization. The employees were encouraged to form different small groups comprising of three to six members in one team, generally from different areas i.e. from marketing, finance, human resource, legal, tax, etc. The different SGAs then used to identify different areas where they would take a challenge of providing a measurable improvement in that particular area that involved exploring and learning various facets for bringing in the desired improvement. For example, if there was some gap in logistics management, the SGA team will take up a goal to set up a standard operating procedure to provide a solution to that goal, and that would involve learning all the facts of legal- or tax-related provisions, as any change in billing or shipping location may have an impact from sales tax/VAT perspective or custom duties or tax impact.

I have one more example of learning by taking challenges in one other organization where there was another kind of challenge and reward mechanism. The organization had different values as principles for running its business, like resourcefulness, compliances, and teamwork. Every year, the company used to choose five to six teams out of more than 50 such nomination and give them a "Values in Action" award for showing excellence in the different values. This approach prompted the individuals and teams to keep learning the best ways to deliver measurable impact and improvement in multiple areas of business.

But why does creating challenges work?

Introducing challenges in learning makes the learning secondary. The participants focus more on winning the challenges, and are ready to upgrade their learning for the purposes of excelling in that challenge. The feelings of satisfaction and accomplishment in winning the challenge takes the driver seat and learning happens as a natural progression. Learning become a necessary tool to win the challenge.

If you have some experience of working with corporate, you'd have already noticed that corporate trainings and team activities these days are much more oriented towards introducing challenges, which in turn enhances human learning and performance. Hence, gamification and introducing challenges do have the great potential to enhance the quality and pace of learning.

You may try some strategies or use some apps stated in this chapter to boost your learning.

Chapter 7: Learning by Teaching (Including Technology)

****

"While we teach, we learn" ~ *Seneca*

For centuries, it is well-known that one of the best ways to learn is by way of teaching others. But now scientists from last few decades have been researching why this method works so well.

It is because explaining something to other person requires you to retrieve the information on the subject from your memory. It requires you to arrange your thoughts about the subject in your memory clearly. You have to be able to explain it simply. Albert Einstein once stated, "If you can't explain it simply enough, it means you have not yet understood it yourself."

Scientists conducted research and found that students who were asked to tutor others work harder to understand the subject material, recall it more accurately and apply it more effectively in teaching others. Scientists term this learning technique as "Protégé Effect." Protégé is a person who is guided and supported by an older and more experienced or influential person. There was evidence that the students who learned by teaching others scored comparatively higher than those who had just learned only for themselves.

There are studies[13] that also show that the older siblings are more intelligent compared to their younger siblings and have a higher IQ as they teach their younger siblings the things they need to learn.

The scientists at Stanford University have developed a cutting edge tool for learning by teaching, and they call it a teaching agent. This teaching agent is a virtual computer system that can learn, ask questions, and give feedback just like a normal student. Scientists have developed this teachable agent and call it *Betty's Brain*[14], which has learned thousands of hours of subject information, which is

13

http://science.sciencemag.org/content/316/5832/1717
[14] https://www.learntechlib.org/p/76357/

taught to it by numerous high school students.

When the students are teaching these teachable agents, their own understanding becomes much clearer, as they try to organize their thoughts in their head cohesively, recalling from their memory in order to explain the virtual brain well. The 2009 study of Betty's Brain published in one journal that the students engaged in learning by way of teaching had spent more time going over the study material and learned it more thoroughly.

Scientists have found that the feedback from the teachable agents further enhances the tutors' learning. The agent's questions force the users to think and explain the material in their own way, and watching the agent solve problems (based on learning from the tutors) allows users to see their knowledge put into action.

In 2009, researchers at Stanford University studied a group of fifth grade students. One group was asked to learn for themselves, the other group was asked to teach virtual pupils, or teachable agents (TAs). The results were interesting; they found that students didn't display the same ownership over their own learning as they did with the TAs. The group working with the TAs was "much more emotionally connected to the learning process."

The results of another study[15] revealed that students learning by preparing to teach intervention developed a more detailed and better-organized concept map of the problem compared with other students. Such student were also noted to be engaged in more metacognitive processing strategies and had higher levels of mathematics problem solving achievement compared with other students who simply learned for their own purposes.

The Protégé Effect helps students learn better because of the following reasons:

- Expecting to teach others encourages the student to learn in a more structured way, so that they can seek out key pieces of

15

http://psycnet.apa.org/doiLanding?doi=10.1037%2Fedu0000071

information out of the material they have learned.

- Learning with the intent of teaching often prompts the student to use additional techniques beyond those used when learning for yourself, which leads to a more comprehensive understanding of the material.

- Expecting to teach also increases the motivation to learn, meaning that students generally make a greater effort to learn for those that they will teach, than they do for themselves. They try to understand the information well, and discover gaps in their own understanding of the subject.

The importance of teaching to learn is gaining acceptance amongst educators. The educators are creating situations where the students can teach other students to learn better. One example is at University of Pennsylvania[16], where they have a

---

[16] https://www.fastcompany.com/3013734/why-

"cascading mentoring program" in which college undergraduates teach computer science to high school students, who in turn teach further to middle school students.

How teaching is the most effective way to understand a concept was succinctly summed up by Aristotle:

"Those who know, do; those who understand, teach"

Therefore, go out, find someone who needs some knowledge of any concept you know better and teach him. This will help you solidify your understanding of the concept.

If you want your learning to go to highest levels, and you are sincere in becoming an expert in your field, you will find the information in the next chapter valuable, which is entirely focused on building your expertise in any field you choose to work.

---

teaching-makes-you-smarter

Chapter 8: Accelerate Your Learning To Become An Expert

****

"An expert is a man who has made all the mistakes which can be made, in a narrow field." ~ Niels Bohr

Learning enables us to lead an enriched and fulfilled life, as we are able put the acquired knowledge to work for us. There is a quote by Frank A. Clark that goes like this: "The more you learn, the more you earn."

An adult human brain is around three pounds i.e. around 2% of the total body weight. But small size and weight doesn't matter because the world rewards those people most, who use their brains effectively. People who work by hand have a limit to earn, but people who use their brain have no limit to create endless earning resources in their life. People who work at McDonalds, or who work as a laborer at a construction site, all have a meager hourly wage for manual labor, but people who use their brains and keep on learning and enhancing their mental faculties always maintain the potential to earn more and lead a better lifestyle.

In the previous sections, we talked about various ways to learn better as proven by researchers. We also learned about the myths of the learning style. In the current section, we will talk about the ways in which you can upgrade your learning capabilities to the next levels and reach the top and become an expert in your field.

Everyone loves to reach the summit of his chosen pursuit. You would want to become an expert in your field, wouldn't you? You would want to upgrade your skills to attain higher levels in your chosen pursuits. You would want to be an authority in your field, because authority brings autonomy and freedom to live life on your own terms. You want people to come to you for your expert knowledge and advice.

In this section, you will learn a few ways that will help you to improve your learning potential and help you to become an expert in your chosen field. But before we talk about that, remember you have to start the journey from the point where you are standing currently. You need to know what level of learning you are currently at. Therefore, let's look at a few methodologies to assess the level of your existing stage of learning.

Four Stages for Learning Any New Skills

In human psychology, there are four stages of learning that transition an individual from the state of incompetence to competence in any skill. It was initially described as "Four Stages for Learning Any New Skills" and the theory was developed by Noel Burch in 1970. This theory is also often referred to as the **Competency Ladder** from the perspective of acquiring new skills.

The theory explains that initially when we start to learn anything, we even don't know what we don't know. It is worth repeating. Yes, we even don't know what we don't know and that keeps most people stuck like a frog in the well who doesn't know what the ocean looks like. At this level of competency, it is very difficult to even fathom the thought of a different world, because we are not able to relate to that world. But when we become aware about our incompetence, we work on improving those skills and soon we learn and consciously act in a competent manner. With enough practice, we become so competent that we are even unconscious of our competence, and that's the last stage of competence, where competent behavior becomes your second nature.

Let's try to understand each of these levels.

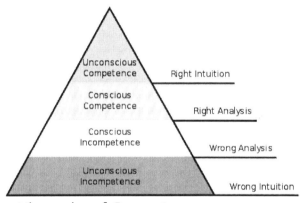

Hierarchy of Competence

(Image courtesy: wikipedia)

1. Unconscious Incompetence

At this stage, the individual does not understand or know how to do something and does not necessarily recognize the deficiency in his learning. He or she may even deny the usefulness of the skill. This stage requires that the individual must recognize their own incompetence and the value of the new skill before moving on to the next stage. The length of time an individual spends in this stage depends on the strength of the stimulus to learn. Either he has to be motivated to learn, if it is a voluntary learning, or if it is a job requirement, then there must be a fear of punishment as a stimulus. There is no or very low scope of using intuition to handle the task at this stage.

2. Conscious Incompetence

The next stage of evolution is increase in awareness by getting deeper into the subject. In this stage of conscious incompetence though, the individual does not understand or know how to do something. He does recognize the deficit in his learning, as well as the value of a new skill in addressing the deficit. Being mindful of the incompetence and the requirement of skill, the individual starts to put efforts into learning. The making of mistakes can be integral to the learning process at this stage, meaning the learner would mostly not be in a position to rightly analyze the correct action in this stage.

3. Conscious Competence

In the next stage, the individual understands or knows how to do something. By putting efforts, making mistakes in the earlier stage, the individual is now competent at this stage, but demonstrating the skill or knowledge requires concentration. It may be broken down into steps, and there is heavy conscious involvement in executing the new skill. The learner is able to make the right analysis of situation, thanks to his or her efforts and concentration on the process.

4. Unconscious Competence

This is the final stage of mastering any skills. Before reaching this stage, the individual has already put so much time into practicing a skill that it has become "second nature" and can be performed easily. As a result, the skill can be performed while executing another task.

This is because skill has become a part of the sub-conscious mind, and it doesn't require active involvement of your brain. Here, you are so competent that you are even unconscious about your competence. Now, you have arrived in the category of expert, where you intuitively know what is the right action to be taken in any given situation, given that you have handled a vast variety of similar situations already.

To understand the four stages of competence, let's take an example of learning to drive a car.

Initially, you were even not aware of what you don't know. Only if you have strong stimulus to learn i.e. you want to independently travel on your own, then only you would want to put efforts in learning to drive the car. You commit mistakes in driving, maybe getting some minor scratches or dent is the cost you pay for learning in this second stage. Now you drive with competence, but you actively concentrating on when to apply brakes or when to put the accelerator on—you are consciously competent. Then you reach the last stage where you even don't need to pay any attention to the car's function. You wouldn't even think about putting the key into the ignition. You wouldn't even realize that the car is already speeding on the highway, and you are comfortably chatting with your accompanying colleague or friend, without there being any need of conscious effort to drive the car. Here, you have achieved the stage of unconscious competence.

Dreyfus Model of Skill Acquisition
There is another study by two brothers Stuart and Hubert Dreyfus about the levels of acquiring competence. This model is famously known as **Dreyfus's Model of Skill Acquisition** in the field of education and operations research. It focuses on explaining how students acquire skills through formal instructions and practice. They proposed this model in 1980 in a report on their research at University of California, Berkeley. The report proposes that any individual goes through five different stages of learning:

1. Novice
This is the first stage of learning. Here, the individual doesn't know anything about the

subject. In this stage, he has to adopt the process of rigid adherence to the taught rules or plans.

There is no exercise of discretionary judgment at this stage. Here, the student needs to spend enough time in understanding the rules of learning in that particular area.

2. Advanced Beginner

As the novice begins to cope with real situations and develops an understanding of the relevant context of operation in the area of learning, the next step comes when he starts to take note of the additional aspects of the situation or domain.

The advance beginner starts to get the perception of the situation that he is facing. Since the individual has just started to get the hold of the rules, he must spend enough time in learning the rules yet.

3. Competent

Competence develops when the individual develops organizing principles to quickly access the particular rules that are relevant to the specific task at hand; hence, competence is characterized by actively choosing a course of action.

Here, the individual starts handling multiple tasks and keeps on accumulating more and more information. He deliberately plans the work and formulates the routine as well for the activities. At this stage the individual develops competency, so he should spend most of the time practicing what he has learned with lesser time needed in learning or remembering the rules.

4. Proficiency

Now, the learner gets the holistic view of the situation. He understands all the rules and knows when to apply different rules. He is aware about the interplay between the various rules and the impact of the outcomes from the decisions to be taken by him. The learner is now able to prioritize the actions well.

He is now very much involved in the actions, as compared to the previous stages. By enough practice, he now doesn't need to again refer to rules as in the case of novice or advance beginner; with the force of involvement, he is now ready for skill enhancement.

5. **Expert**

This is the ultimate level of learning. Here, the individual transcends from his reliance on rules, maximums, and guidelines. Rather he develops intuitive grasp of situations based on his deep tacit understanding based on experience of various scenarios handled due to practice. As noted in the previous theory of Hierarchy of competence, this stage is equivalent to the unconscious competence, and your intuition is strongly developed to make quick decisions.

While the **proficient performer** based on his immersion in the skillful activities sees what needs to be done, he needs to yet decide what needs to be done. But the **expert performer** not only see what needs to be done, he, based on his vast repertoire of situational discriminations can immediately decide how to achieve that goal. Thus, the ability to make the subtle and refined distinction between the actions to be taken in different situations makes the expert performer, setting him apart from merely a proficient performer. This level is the apex level, and therefore one need to put efforts to keep practicing to maintain such skills to make all his decisions largely unconscious and effortless.

I believe you would have noted enough symptoms of learners at different stages and probably would have made some assessment of your own level of competency. Unless you already find yourself as an expert in any area, now is the time you would ask what specifically it would need and how much time it takes to become an expert in your identified pursuits. This is what we will address now.

How You can Become An Expert

Most people have probably already heard about the 10,000-hour rule to become an expert.

If not, the 10,000-hour rule had its genesis in a study conducted by K. Anders Ericsson, professor of psychology from the University of Florida. He researched a lot of top athletes, musician, and chess players out there in the world to research what it takes to become an expert in one's chosen field.

Based on his research, he noted that few top musicians took around 10,000 hours to become expert in their field. It so happened, that few musicians started so early in their life to start playing their instrument, and by the time they spent 10,000 hours practicing their craft, they had become masters in their craft.

By the way, even 10,000 hours is not a small period. It is equivalent to spending five years in a full-time job. Just do this simple calculation: you put *forty* hours in a week to work, and you work *fifty* weeks in a year (assuming you get 2 weeks of vacations), that makes it 2,000 hours in one year, and therefore 10,000 hours of practice means five years spent in a full-time job.

Now taking this research of Ericsson as a basis, Malcolm Gladwell, in his bestseller book *"Outlier: The Story Of Success,"* covered this 10,000-hour rule in his book. His version of this rule in his book was seemingly indicating as if becoming an expert in any field is subject to some objective criterion of timelines i.e. spend 10,000 hours and become expert in anything you want. It became popular in way that 10,000 hours was considered some magical number and by the time one devotes these many hours, he or she is guaranteed to be an expert.

However, there is another side of the story, which many people are not aware about. And this other part of the story comes from the main researcher Ericsson. One press release reported[17] that Gladwell likely drew his conclusion of 10,000-hour rule in his book based on a Ericsson's paper, where forty violinists in Germany were studied to get more details about how much time it takes to reach their level of expertise. The researchers of the paper primarily explored the multiple factors that differentiated the best musicians from the good or the mediocre ones. It was found in the research that the top two groups of violinists spent significantly more time practicing than the others. But there were people who spend

---

[17] https://www.businessinsider.in/A-top-psychologist-says-theres-only-one-way-to-become-the-best-in-your-field-but-not-everyone-agrees/articleshow/52715262.cms

more time or even less time than that. In a nutshell, there was no specific finding about the number of hours, rather the paper cited multiple factors leading to gaining expertise by these violinists.

The release reported that Ericsson, the original researcher of the paper, stated that the 10,000-hour rule criterion popularized by Gladwell, couldn't be an objective test that could be applied to any skill uniformly. He stated that there can't be any objective or magical number of hours that would mean a guarantee to become an expert. It is not only the number of hours that matter. Ericsson stated that 10,000 hours of merely repeating the same activity does not turn anyone into an expert immediately[18].

And yes, it makes sense. Merely doing same thing every year for a period of 20 years cannot be stated as carrying an experience of 20 years. It could be merely one year of experience just repeated for a period of 20 years.

---

[18] http://www.bbc.com/future/story/20121114-gladwells-10000-hour-rule-myth

Therefore, this principle of 10,000 hours is not a sacrosanct principle or a magical number that is uniformly applicable to all skills.

Rather Ericsson explains that deliberate practice is something that makes someone an expert in his chosen pursuits. Ericsson explains that there are three different types of practices that people follow, but it is only deliberated practice that matters, if you sincerely want to become an expert of your chosen pursuit. You will find these different practices and the concept of becoming an expert already covered in my other book *The Science of High Performance*, where I have covered many other scientific principles and techniques for enhancing performance.

Precisely, Ericsson explains that there are three types of practices, which people pursue to gain any skill in any field, as stated below:

a. Naive Practice
b. Purposeful Practice
c. Deliberate Practice

Let's look at each of these one by one and learn why Ericsson emphasizes that only deliberate practice is the way to attaining the status of expert or master of any particular field.

1. **Naive practice** means a generic kind of mindless practice, where you simply keep on doing what you had learned earlier. It's like always being in the performance zone and just taking actions only based on your existing knowledge and skillset without any focus or intention of improvement. This type of practice of doing the same thing repeatedly and expecting that it will improve does not work at all.

It is like playing guitar from your college days until your forties without deliberately learning the best ways to press the right nodes and strings—and expecting that the 20 years of practice will make you a better guitarist. You don't get the exact benefit of the feature of adaptability of human body and mind by repeating the same thing mindlessly over and over again.

Then what makes the difference?

2. **Purposeful Practice**: This is a better way to practice and learn a skill faster, as compared to naive practice, though a level below the deliberate practice. Here are the features of a purposeful practice:

   a. Purposeful practice has well-defined and specified goals. Take the example of any sports training or learning any new language or playing any musical instrument within a particular time frame. Here, you have a clear objective to learn a skill in a particular time frame.

   b. Purposeful practice is focused.

This kind of practice is not like planning a casual trip to your grocery store to wander around and grab something. No, it doesn't work that way. Purposeful practice is not something that is fun or relaxing work. Rather, it is to be entirely focused on that activity. If you are allowing anything and everything to disturb you in that activity, that's not a focused practice—you will end up wasting your time—and forget about learning anything.

c. Purposeful practice <u>requires feedback.</u>

You need to know how you're doing step by step. Did you miss a note playing that song you want to play perfectly four times in today's practice? <u>Immediate feedback to help you identify what you're doing wrong</u> (and how you can improve) is essential.

d. Purposeful practice wants you to <u>get out of your comfort zone.</u>

This is one of the most important elements of purposeful practice. If you don't push yourself beyond your comfort zone, you will never improve.

Anyone can realize that practicing with well-defined and specific goals, in a focused manner, with an appropriate feedback system about your mistakes, and with consistent pushing beyond the comfort zone—contains all the necessary triggers to improve learning and performance. That's why purposeful practice is certainly a great way to learn anything new. But there is something more that works wonders when it comes to practicing and seeking high performance, and that's called deliberate practice.

3. **Deliberate Practice:** That's called a gold standard of any practice. This practice has all the elements of the purposeful practice, but it additionally has the element of coaching or teaching added to it through a clear training program in the established field.

Deliberate practice involves the pursuit of personal improvement via well-defined, specific goals and targeted areas of expertise, as required in purposeful practice. Additionally, it requires a teacher or coach who has demonstrated an ability to help others improve the desired area of expertise—say chess, tennis, or music—and who can give continuous feedback.

Think about Tiger Woods, the titan of golf. Do you think he needs any training or coaching for golf? He hired a swing coach for a long period of time to correct his swing. He knew very well an expensive club set wouldn't make him win the game—

it was the mastery of his craft that would keep him at the apex position. He knows the importance of deliberate practice under expert guidance to consistently improve and master his game.

Ericsson states that just working harder or working more does not seem to be associated with high levels of performance. Rather, if you're working with a teacher or a mentor who has attained this high level of performance, that individual can help you now design the kind of training activities that they may have engaged in order to reach that higher level of performance.

He states: "It's not just a matter of accumulating hours. If you're doing your job, and you're just doing more and more of the same, you're not actually going to get better."

Ericsson succinctly explains how the inner brain structure and neural circuit changes with deliberate practice in below words:

> The main thing that sets experts apart from the rest of us is that their years of practice have changed the neural circuitry in their brains to

produce highly specialized mental representations, which in turn make possible the incredible memory, pattern recognition, problem-solving, and other sorts of advanced abilities needed to excel in their particular specialties. The more you study a subject, the more detailed your mental representations of it become, and the better you get at assimilating new information.

I loved his wonderful thought, where he says:

"There is no reason not to follow your dream. Deliberate practice can open the door to a world of possibilities that you may have been convinced were out of reach. Open that door."

I hope you have gathered enough techniques to help you assess your current level and most importantly this will help you to chart your action plan to reach your destination of knowledge. Last but not least, you have to put in the effort to become successful in any endeavor you choose, the more deliberated practice you do, the better your chances of success.

Closing Thoughts

****

"Always walk through life as if you have something new to learn, and you will." ~ Vernon Howard

Finally, we come to the end of our journey together. I thank you for your time and efforts in learning how to learn better, faster, and in sustainable manner.

I would ask you to pat your back first. Yes, you deserve it. In fact, you are in those selected breed of people who value learning more than anything. Most importantly, your desire to learn effectively will enable you to get maximum rewards in return of your efforts put.

Whether you are a student, corporate employee, professional, or a sincere parent who is looking for an overall growth of their kid, this book is an effort to extract the most relevant content that can help you to accelerate your learning.

Now, this book has come to an end; but as they say every end is the beginning of a new story. Therefore, before closing and putting this book down, make a promise to yourself that next time whenever you pick up something to learn, you will try to use at least a few principles out of this book. I am confident that the science-backed researched techniques covered in this book will help you to meet your learning objectives effectively.

Wishing a more knowledgeable and smarter you!

Cheers

Copyright © 2018 by Som Bathla

All rights reserved. No part of this book may be reproduced in any form without permission in writing from the author.

No part of this publication may be reproduced or transmitted in any form or by any means, mechanical or electronic, including photocopying or recording, or by any information storage and retrieval system, or transmitted by email or by any other means whatsoever without permission in writing from the author.

DISCLAIMER

While all attempts have been made to verify the information provided in this publication, the author does not assume any responsibility for errors, omissions, or contrary interpretations of the subject matter herein.

The views expressed are those of the author alone, and should not be taken as expert instruction or commands. The reader is responsible for his or her own actions.

The author makes no representations or warranties with respect to the accuracy or completeness of the contents of this work and specifically disclaims all warranties, including without limitation warranties of fitness for a particular purpose. No warranty may be created or extended by sales or promotional materials. The advice and recipes contained herein may not be suitable for everyone. This work is sold with the understanding that the author is not engaged in rendering medical, legal or other professional advice or services. If professional assistance is required, the services of a competent professional person should be sought. The author shall not be liable for damages arising here from. The fact that an individual, organization of website is referred to in this work as a citation and/or potential source of further information does not mean that the author endorses the information the individual, organization to website may provide or recommendations they/it may make. Further, readers should be aware that Internet websites listed in this work might have changed or disappeared between when this work was written and when it is read.

Adherence to all applicable laws and regulations, including international, federal, state, and local governing professional licensing, business practices, advertising, and all other aspects of doing business in any jurisdiction in the world is the sole responsibility of the purchaser or reader.

13877070R10090

Made in the USA
Lexington, KY
02 November 2018